BEYOND THE RAINBOW

Precognition and Intuitive Thought

Andrea J Parker

Kindle Amazon

This book is dedicated to my family who have always trusted and believed in me.

Thank you for your continued support.

To my late Mother who I love and miss so much even now.

CONTENTS

INTRODUCTION

I have written this book to share with you, my readers, about my own personal accounts of true events and experiences of precognitive dreams and intuitive thoughts. My decision to share my story is not one I have taken lightly due to it's nature and contents. It has been necessary to allow for some passage of time, before I felt comfortable to do this and I make no apologies for that. For those of you who have an interest in this subject; I ask that you have patience and bear with me as my story unfolds. I hope that any fellow like minded persons can find some solace and comfort in this work, as precognitive dreams can sometimes be very emotional and distressing. I offer my sincere condolences and respect to anyone who has lost loved one's or have been touched in anyway by the events I am about to discuss with you. This work is autobiographical in context and an honest and true account of my experiences.

Beyond The Rainbow

A personal account
of true events

By Andrea Jacqueline Parker.

"Somewhere over the rainbow

Skies are blue

And the dreams that you dare to dream

Really do come true"

BIOGRAPHY.

Or in other words - a little bit about me:

Barbara, my mother, continuously made a point of informing me how my birth had been a little unusual. Of course, she never told tall stories or exaggerated the truth ....It went something like this....On the 30th August 1962 the hospital was full of expectant mums and having "no room at the inn" so to speak, I was born in the hospital's bathroom very premature. I was so small I came out sideward's and slipped into a kidney dish. Apparently; mum craved cornflakes and orange juice during her pregnancy and when I came into the world she said, "I was covered in both". Yuck! And that my friends, is the story she used to tell me when I was a small child. I believed her implicitly. Surprisingly, the first part is very true. I was indeed born prematurely but not too sure about the cornflakes and orange juice?

My parents are Ron and Barbara Foster. I have three siblings and we all owe our survival to science and the technological development of incubators. These were a relatively new development back in the 1960's and so I guess we are all lucky to be here today. Regardless of how I came into existence I am pleased to say; I am the product of a happy and reasonably content childhood.

I have been married to my husband Andy for nearly forty years and have two grown up children, Annabel and Alan. My most recent blessings are my two little grandsons who can be a handful at times but I love them dearly. Recently, my son Alan and his new wife have announced another to be new arrival this year. I am well and truly excited and in grandma mode at this time.

I originate from a predominantly working class background and proud to do so. I have lived in Haxey in the Isles of Axholme until I was fourteen years old and then moved to Scunthorpe in Lincolnshire when my father got a job on the local steelworks. I experienced the usual spotty teenage adolescence and settled down very young compared with today's generation. Married at eighteen years old. OMG! I hear you cry – so young. Not because we had to either! Marriage isn't always the bed of roses you think it's going to be is it? Ok definitely a few moans and groans along the years but on the whole –

no regrets. Remember the red Ford Capri Andy with yellow bucket seats – happy days..... Sorry, just digressing slightly.

My vocation into nursing came later in life when at the age of twenty eight I returned to adult education. I went on to complete my degree in adult nursing and have now specialized in palliative care and hospice work. I knew this was where my passions lay and where I belonged. Nursing involves; a mixture of the sciences, logic, compassion, empathy and most importantly common sense and intuitive thought. A strange combination it seems. With this knowledge and ability I have been able to support others on their physical, emotional and spiritual journeys using a holistic approach to care. I am forever amazed by the tremendous courage and great dignity shown by those patients and families I have cared for.

I am probably more of a spiritual person than a deeply religious one. Although I have faith in myself and my convictions, I often question and reason why things happen in life? I try to look for the logic first in all things. (This is because my star sign is Virgo – so I am told). Lovingly, raised as a Christian I attended regular Sunday school. I say my prayers every night. But I don't feel the need to go to a church every week to feel any presence. A bit hypocritical I know. Just being honest.

I believe there is good and bad in the world just as in ourselves. No one truly knows what drives human-kind to the extremes of evilness or to the higher realms of purity and goodness. We all make our own choices and way in life. No exceptions and no excuses!

PROLOGUE

The "Nitty – Gritty" of what
I really want to talk about:

Perhaps the theories of humankind being descendents of ancient aliens aren't such a myth! I'm not knocking Darwin's theory of evolution either. It's just there are so many unanswered questions, for example: who actually built the pyramids? Could have been ancient man but how did they know the science and technology back then? Maybe we shouldn't be looking at psychic mumbo jumbo but more at the human development of our species and the parts of the brain we have yet to use. Remember the film Extra Terrestrial (E.T) "Out you come". Extra sensory perception is not merely a psychic ability, it is in us all. Some people have yet to open their minds and discover this for themselves! We need to use our brains more – well those parts we have yet to develop. (No pun intended).

If we are true descendents of ancient aliens, then we have already come a long way in our development but it could take thousands or perhaps millions of years before our brains develop to its full potential in the use of extrasensory perception. What some of us are experiencing now is only the beginning. Is it not already possible to travel into the future in our sub consciousness? Just as it is possible to regress and travel back to the past through hypnosis – and why is that theory more acceptable to psychologists and scientists? So many questions and so few answers.

Consider this: what if we were able to tune in to other peoples thoughts, feelings and emotions. A bit like fine tuning on a radio wave. Only the wave travels forward into the future taking you with it for a few moments thus exposing your subconscious to events that have not yet taken place. Perhaps, we are living in a parallel universe? if you believe in that concept of reality and we are able to connect somehow in time to our counterparts? Surreal and scary isn't it. Could it be some form of telepathy? I hear you asking, well who knows! But this is how it feels for me….. This then is my own journey.

I need to confess that at this point, Alan (my son) and I had been watching an awful lot of Ancient Alien and Cosmos DVD'S recently. Morgan Freeman's voice is still lingering in my ears now. In knowing this may have influenced my thoughts on this section we still need to consider all theories or perhaps you disagree.

In parapsychology, precognition is also called future sight and second sight. It is a type of extra sensory perception that would involve the acquisition or effect of future information that cannot be deduced from presently available and normally acquired sense-based information or laws of physics or nature. Premonitions provide information about future events that is perceived as emotion.

Scientists over the years have struggled to explain these phenomena because of the complexities' involved in understanding extrasensory perception (ESP). The principle of "cause and effect" in the world of science becomes turned upside down as the concept of precognition tends to disproves the theory, that an effect cannot occur before its cause.

Mind boggling stuff isn't it! However; history records many occurrences of precognition through dreams, visions or those déjà vu moments we all experience from time to time. Even, old Aristotle examined the phenomenon of dreams and precognition in his "On Divination in Sleep." Dreams are a connection to our human subconscious that creates images, ideas, emotions and sensations occurring involuntary in the mind during sleep. Little wonder scientists remain skeptical. How do you explain the unexplained and hey! I'm certainly no expert on that either. The unexplained I mean.........You know the affirmation of our existence or the big question we ask ourselves from time to time..... Why are we here? and what is the meaning of life? Whoops! Sorry that's two questions.

Yes! I dare say, there are a lot of people out there who claim to be clairvoyant and psychic posing as mediums raking in the dosh, but we need to accept that there are also many genuine people who have a natural ability to foresee events. Perhaps only glances of the future or fleeting moments of images and feelings. The experience feels real, even though one cannot explain how it has materialized in their minds eye. So how did this phenomenon begin for me.............

At the tender age of eight years old it was as if a switch had turned a light on in my brain and opened it up to new thoughts and emotions. Intuition became more enhanced and I experienced more precognitive dreams leading to those Déjà vu moments in life. *Enlightenment had occurred*. Time was a parallel universe including; the past, present and future. I began to recall my dreams more frequently and later in life would become analytical of them trying to decipher what messages they were conveying. It seems to me that most of the answers we seek are deep within us if we only open our minds eye to our sub-consciousness. Dreams are a way of analysing our lives and often provide us with the answers we are looking for.

Having said that; strangely enough, I am still me. I haven't turned into some psychic freak. I am probably more in tune with myself and reality than I have ever been. One thing I have noticed over the years is the existence of what I call a "three week window" Especially with precognitive dreams predicting future events. Any dream where I have foreseen images of

events usually prove real after approximately this time. Of course I don't remember all my dreams but the ones that have affected me or caused emotional disturbance may linger longer in my memory.

So why write this book now? Well I think it's time to tell my story. I am just an ordinary, average everyday person just like you but there have been too many coincidences and events in my life that ring true. To the extent of questioning my own sanity at times. No I'm o.k. not crazy or delusional. I remain sane and fully grounded - I hope. You can be the judge of that. All I ask is that you keep an open mind.

Another reason is the fact I'm not getting any younger and at present I can remember events clearly as if it was yesterday – might not be able to in a few years time. Also, I want my family and children to truly know me. Not just the snippets of stories I may have told them over the years often watching their faces in bewilderment. I am not ashamed of who I am or of what I have seen.

Some precognitive dreams and events have been disturbing and I have wanted to wish them away. Often wondering why show me these things when I have no control or power to change them..... With this in mind, the last thing I've ever wanted to do is cause upset or distress to anyone, especially if they have lost loved ones. Unfortunately; I can make no apologies for any connections with true life events. It is what it is. This is an honest account. Read on if you will........

◆ ◆ ◆

THE BEGINNING

As a child I was always a happy dreamer and felt a little bit different from others. I could always drift off into my own little world full of imagination, seeing faces and images in clouds and feel like I was flying in my sleep. Oh! and sometimes dream about things before they happened. Of course everyone is capable of such feats or so I thought. My mother used to say, "Our Andrea could go to sleep on a clothes line". Never quite knew what she meant by that at the time. I loved to recall my dreams and wasn't surprised at the many déjà vu moments I experienced even then. Of course I just thought everyone did this and that it was normal.

I remember when I was about seven years old sharing a twin bedroom with my older sister. This was when we were living in the village of Haxey. Oh! Happy times growing up. However; I do vividly recall she gave me a right belt on the nose once after a pillow fight there was blood all over the white pillow cases. We sneaked the evidence into the wash as we knew we'd both get into bother – seems there was some sibling rivalry then - so pretty normal childhood.

Moving onto a more serious note. Around this time I had my first "Out of body" experience. (I'm pretty sure this wasn't due to the smack on the nose, just before you say it yourself) I know now that this is what happened but as a young child I just thought I was having delightful floating dreams.

On more than one occasion in a dream state; I recall opening the bedroom window and looking out over the back garden and country fields. I experienced, such a feeling of wonderment and awe with the world. How beautiful and warm it felt to me, inside and out. It was like stepping into familiar surroundings but in a different time. The rest of the world was asleep only I was there. I felt safe, but it didn't look quite the same. The colours of the landscape had a dull green and blue overtone to them. This I do remember and thought it strange. I wasn't alarmed by it. I flew out of the window like a bird gliding around the garden, swooping and swaying in the breeze looking down on familiar places. The feeling of peace and freedom was immense. The strangest thing was floating over by body which was sleeping in my bed and looking down upon myself before my spirit set off to play – well I can only describe how it seemed at the time to a child aged seven.

Was it a way of escaping the real world I hear you asking, well of course it was!

Is there a logical explanation to this conundrum? My parents probably would have said yes there is. You see many a night I awoke with a sudden tug at my legs only to look up hazily from my sleep to see my dad pulling my wellingtons from my feet. How funny is that? Of course I just looked at him smiled and nodded off back to "Cloud cuckoo" land in my sleep. Apparently; according to my parents I used to sleepwalk and you must know it is dangerous to awaken anyone in that state and so they would just follow me outside. We only had one outside toilet back then in the 1960's so needs were a must I'm afraid. Unless mum had put a pee pot or bucket on the upstairs landing. Oh yes they were the days; haven't times changed. So logically you may argue that in fact I was merely sleep walking and that this is not uncommon amongst young children trying to escape the pressures of growing up.

Not convinced! Well I'm not so sure either. So many unanswered questions like - could I have entered the astral plane? What the heck is it anyway?

According to literature on the subject: just looking at Wikipedia, the free encyclopedia LoL. The astral plane is also called the astral world, is a plane of existence. It is a world of planetary spheres crossed by the soul in its astral body on the way to being born and after death. It is said to be populated by angels, spirits and other immaterial beings. Occult teachings tell us that the astral plane can be visited through astral projection, meditation and mantra, near death experience, lucid dreaming or other means. Astral projection author Robert Bruce describes the astral as seven planes that take the form of planar surfaces separated by coloured zones. Higher planes have bright colourful patterns whereas lower planes appear far duller. Similar to my own experience.

As humans our consciousness is focused on the physical plane of our existence. This is often a survival tactic. We choose to ignore that which we don't understand or as my husband would say, "If I can't see it for myself then I don't believe it". In the physical world seeing is believing. No wonder everyone is skeptical. Theorists of parapsychology believe that the physical plane was set up for learning purposes only. You are in a physical existence to learn and understand that your energy, translated into thoughts, feelings and emotions cause all experience. Remember our previous discussions about "Cause and effect" in the world of science, surely then we cannot ignore this also occurs on other levels or planes to which our consciousness might transcend.

In our sleep we can explore other planes because we are not restricted by our physical being. Our minds are then free to wander the realms. Is this a simple enough explanation for you! Awe well! Probably not but sounds good. Did I visit the astral plane I'd certainly like to think so as it is more comforting than the explanation of sleep walking?

KNOWING

*(In memory of my
dear grandma)*

Grandma Hunt was my mum's mother and she could be a little scary and intimidating sometimes, I remember. Very much working class. She had supported my granddad from his humble upbringings of working hard down the coal mines near Doncaster to the reputable builder of council houses in the Isle of Axholme. A small family firm but still quite an achievement in the 1970's. My own father worked for him for many years before going into the steelwork trade in Scunthorpe..... Many happy times travelling in granddads Zepha four car (least think that was what it was) going to Gainsborough fish market for our "finny haddock" for lunch on a Friday. Usually my sister and I accompanied them. Mum used to work typing and doing other various office jobs to help the business back then.

I used to call and see grandma on the way home from school. I was about eight years old at that time. Grandma was in her mid to late fifties – never sure of her true age but I am told she was only fifty six when she died. I believe she died of heart failure. Unfortunately, she was a heavy smoker and I remember she always looked older than her years.

I remember walking into the house which was like an old cottage style property, always smelt a bit fusty. I went into the kitchen which was sparse and felt cold to me sending shivers down my spine. Grandma met me in the doorway leading into the lounge. I looked closely at her. I just knew something was wrong with her although, she looked and sounded familiar. She was more breathless I recall but at eight years old that didn't particularly mean anything to me.

I instantly experienced an over whelming feeling of impending loss. I knew that today would be the last time I would ever see her. I wanted to hug her forever to say goodbye and don't be frightened grandma but I couldn't.

Although, she clearly loved her grandchildren dearly, she was a very "matter of fact person" and didn't do soppy hugs and kisses only when really needed. Life had made her quite hard I think. It took all my energy and strength not to cry and I appeared my cheery self when she asked me to run an errand.

Typical grandma very much like my own mum. Always, "robbing Peter to pay Paul" so to speak. Despite the family firms profits grandma never had much money in her own purse. She wanted me to pop to see her friend who lived up the other end of the village and take a present for the grandson with a hand written note. I didn't know what the note contained. It was in fact to ask to borrow a fiver so she could go to bingo that evening. She loved her bingo and my sister and I often went with her. Grandma could be a right laugh sometimes. I was going to miss her! I remember dashing on my old bike to run the errand really only wanting to get back to her quickly to see her again whilst I had the opportunity to do so.

Upon my return she met me in the kitchen again and I gave her the message her friend had sent and the five pound note. She then told me to get myself off straight home. I vaguely remember giving her a small hug and kiss on the cheek as I felt I needed to do this but of course she chastised me for being so daft and sent me on my way.

> *After that I didn't feel sad anymore because I felt she was going to be at peace with herself.*

I sensed physical living was a struggle for her. I'm

not sure how I became aware of that at such a young age but her episodes of coughing and breathlessness had become more frequent. I never found out if she got to bingo that night. I peddled home as fast as I could and remember thinking don't be frightened grandma because you're going to heaven.

There was no sadness in my heart because at such a young age I thought heaven was a nice place for her to be.

My older sister who was ten years old and I shared a twin bedroom and so often one could not awaken without waking the other. The next morning my sister was anxious because she could hear mum crying downstairs and was wondering what the commotion was. As we crept down the steep stairs and entered the living room, I noticed my younger siblings watching television oblivious of events. Mum and Dad were in the kitchen. Dad was trying to console my mother but she was angry and upset. I think it was dad who told us the news that Grandma Hunt had died suddenly during the night. My sister started to cry uncontrollably in the passageway; being older she understood more the physical permanence of death. I took her hand and said, "Why are you crying" she replied, "grandma's died" I answered, "but she has gone to heaven and that's not a sad place". I was too young to fully understand their feelings of loss and grief at that time.

Having lost our own mother eleven years ago I can honestly say, I understand those feelings now in adulthood through my own personal experiences and my work at the hospice. When I reflect on this episode in my life I realize that this was the moment when my mind opened for the first time and intuitive thoughts, feelings and emotions became part my life. The "sixth sense".

I felt no sadness in my loss I was relieved she was at peace. I wasn't sure if I was supposed to feel differently as I watched my family crumble with grief and emotion around me. Being older and wiser now I know how heartbreaking it is to lose a parent. It was especially hard for my mum who needed her own mother and was so young herself at that time.

Mum insisted we saw grandma "laid out" in the front parlour of her home to say our goodbyes. I didn't particularly like this but was the custom at that time. I'd never felt so scared before. The smell of embalming fluid and death lingered in the air and engrossed my nostrils making me feel sick and light headed. Grandma slept in a fine wooden coffin but it didn't look like her. It was her physical being only as I knew her spirit had already flown. This was certainly a reality check! I remember wanting to run out of that room but kept quiet because mum seemed to need us there with her..... I could feel her pain and consequently did not want to upset her further.

God Bless you grandma and rest in peace. xxx

THE ACCIDENTS

There have been many déjà vu moments in my life it would be impossible to recall all of them. This event I am about to narrate holds a very vivid memory for me. It could quite easily have led to my non-existence or in other words my death. Fortunately the quirkiness and divine intervention of fate dealt me a different hand that day – perhaps! Or was I just lucky? Things could have been so different. I am forever indebted…..

At ten years old my sister and I were often sent to stay with our Grandma Phyllis in the village of Reedness near Goole. She was our father's mother and lived with her brother who we knew as Uncle Andy. We loved going to stay there it was always exciting and fun. Happy memories!

A few weeks earlier before our visit I had experienced a strange dream. I remembered it because it was disturbing and I had woken up startled and frightful from my sleep. In the dream I was crossing the road to go into my grandma's garden feeling for some reason excited and eager to get across the road quickly. I turn suddenly and a green van; one of the old Morris minor's with wooden edgings on the door frames is "screeching" and breaking to a halt. It stops abruptly touching my left hip and I lean into it putting my hand on the car bonnet to steady myself. I could feel the metal and the heat from the car engine.

The driver was an elderly man. He alighted from the car staring at me and after a few minutes he starts moaning about having smashed his eggs in the van – then I awoke! Eh! So what on earth was that all about? Nearly got knocked down by a car and all the old man could do was moan about his ruddy eggs! I tried not to dwell on it and over the coming three weeks slowly forgot about it. Please remember at ten years old I had no understanding of extra sensory perception or precognitive dreams.

A few weeks later our family had spent the weekend at Grandma Phyllis's house in Reedness. We had all taken the local bus into the town of Goole to hit the shops. (Well what few shops there were?) I remember it was a bright sunny day and I felt happy and carefree. Dad was always warning his children not to cross the road until the bus was clearly out the way in case of oncoming traffic. I usually remembered and adhered to this sensible piece of advice from my parents. But as we alighted from the bus and I looked over to the other side of the road, I saw that in the garden my Uncle and Aunty along with our cousins were waiting to greet us.

The local bus always dropped us off outside grandma's house in those days – ahh! Village life.......
In my excitement to see them, as soon as, I heard the bus pulling away, I ran forward over the road to meet them. I was only focused on that one thing. I was oblivious to events and hadn't seen the green Morris Minor car on the other side of the road. I heard a loud "screeching" noise as the old man hit the brakes. It was scary and just as in my dream the car stops in the nick of time touching the left side of my body as I reach my hand onto its bonnet to steady myself. My life literally "flashed" before my eyes. I remembered my dream. Everything was exactly the same. I began to shake with shock! I froze to the spot and couldn't move holding on to the bonnet of that dammed car. Oh yes! And Lo and behold out steps the old man never asking if I was o.k. and starts moaning about his delivery of farm eggs which were probably all smashed now. I couldn't quite believe that!

Dad went to the back of the van to help him check for damaged eggs. I found myself being told off for causing the accident or thankfully the "near miss" as it turned out to be. All I really wanted was a hug and for someone to tell me it was alright. Once everyone had stopped fussing about the elderly couple in the Morris minor – I now realize in my maturity that they were in shock too as I remember the old lady in the passenger seat being offered a cup of tea by my grandma.

When my aunty then realised I was still shaking due to the ordeal, she came and took my hand telling, everyone to stop moaning and sat me down in the lounge. I had a lovely cup of sweet tea – which, I eagerly drank and eventually I calmed down. I knew that mum and dad were only cross because of what could have happened to me. However; my brother and sister found it hilariously funny that I'd been so…. told off!

Everything had seemed surreal as if it had been played in slow motion. How could I have dreamt it previously and what did that mean? – At such a young age I had no answers to these frustrating questions – and that began to torment me a little.

So how do you explain it! Over the years I have reflected and retraced events in my life many times as I often do with my dreams; seeking answers. Was it a dream or remote viewing? Why me? I endeavor not to be skeptical and remain open minded. All I ask is that you continue to do the same……….

◆ ◆ ◆

In more recent years there have probably been at least another two episodes in my life involving accidents with a vehicle and a family member. Obviously, I find any precognitive dreams or intuitive thoughts about close family members difficult and disturbing, depending on the content and how it affects my own emotions. I don't particularly want to know all the doom and gloom stuff and in hindsight who would – how would you cope with that responsibility? The knowing. Never being able to change the inevitability of future events.

The only way I have coped with this is to "block" out insightful thoughts; well at least to try and prevent them if they involve family – for the sake of my own sanity. Unfortunately, sometimes the dreams, thoughts and feelings, creep in of their own free will and I have no control over this.

When my son Alan was sixteen and my daughter Annabel was then eighteen years old, Andy and I

decided to take our first holiday aboard withou..
the kids. Hooray! No! Only joking. Even when I was
booking our holiday to Spain my "gut feeling" was,
it'll never come off something will happen to prevent us from going. I think many mums would feel
like that so I decided not to be so negative in
my thoughts. I continued the holiday planning but
within me was a great fear and trepidation about
what was to come. I ignored it convincing myself
not to be so silly.

A few weeks before the holiday I was busy with
housework when from nowhere a thought came
into my mind. It was my own voice speaking. The
words were,

> *"Knowing our luck Alan will get knocked off
> his moped and break his leg probably a week be-
> fore we go on holiday".*

 I gasped! at such a negative thought coming into
my mind, trying to dismiss it. Of course I couldn't.
I remember nagging poor Alan everyday to be care-
ful on his moped and to go steady don't take any
unnecessary risks on his bike or show off with his
mates etc.... He just laughed it off telling me not to
worry so much – he was fine.

I decided to look at things logically examining the
probability or possibility of this accident happening at all. I decided that; although such a thing

was certainly possible it was not probably going to happen at such the precise time as I had envisaged, because that would be too surreal. (That is to say: exactly a week before we were due to go on holiday). With this in mind I got on with the routine of my daily life but the thought hung over me like a black cloud churning at my insides. I loved my children dearly and as any mother wouldn't want any harm to come to them.

We were due to fly to Spain in the early hours of Friday morning. The tickets were booked and back up plans made at home leaving Annabel in charge. I remember thinking; if we just get passed the time line of precisely one week prior the holiday – there was a good chance things would be O.K. Still trying to convince myself even then.....

The Friday evening - just hours under the one week timescale - before our holiday - I made the mistake of thinking Alan was safe. If we were flying at six am early next Friday morning then surely if something was going to happen it would be early on the Friday one week before we were due to fly – if that makes any sense at all.

Annabel, and I settled down in the lounge to watch a DVD and eat munchies at about seven in the evening. I felt relaxed for the first time in ages. Alan was out on his moped with his friends but I was not worried because I'd told myself it was now less than a week before our holiday and Alan was safe. Who was

I kidding – just me then! Unexpectedly, I heard a frantic knock at the front door. Fear gripped me and I just knew!

> *It was Alan's friend. He had been travelling with his dad in the car through Ashby when they saw what appeared to be Alan's moped in the middle of the road near the traffic lights. Police and ambulance vehicles blocked the view of the injured person but he was sure it was Alan's moped. He had thankfully, attended to tell me immediately. Alan's friend was accompanied by his dad and they offered to take me to the scene in their car but I refused. I needed to go myself. Of course there was the possibility that he'd got it wrong and it wasn't Alan but I already knew the answer to that question.*

I drove to the accident scene as though in slow motion. Annabel and her boyfriend were with me. Andy was at work. Alan's moped was splayed across the road – police were taking witness statements. My son was in the ambulance. The doors were closed. I pulled up as near as I was able in my car telling a teary Annabel to remain there and telephone dad.

I am a nurse so I knew the fact that the ambulance was still stationary was not a good sign. Either; they were trying to stabilize the patient or they had died? I was desperate to see him. I prayed it was not a serious injury but only the broken leg I had foreseen. That wouldn't' be so bad would it? He'd still be alive. I had never been as frightened in my life as I tentatively knocked on the ambulance door. A young policeman opened it asking who I was, I said; "The boy's mother". He let me into the ambulance.

Oh My God! Imagine my relief when I saw him alive. The paramedics were working on him to stabilize his fractured neck of femur and gain intravenous access to enable pain relief to be given. He was dopey from the analgesia and rather talkative I remember, trying to explain how the accident had happened. Thank goodness he was only setting off from the traffic lights and therefore travelling at a slow speed before impact otherwise it could have been a very different tale to tell you now. Bless him! He had to stay in hospital for a week and undergo invasive surgery to have an internal fixator put insitu to stabilize the fracture. After being provided with some physiotherapy and a pair of crutches he was discharged home. Then the real work began because he had to learn to walk again. A very brave son. Yes it could have been much worse and I am eternally grateful It wasn't so......

Once again I remain open minded. Although I have felt skepticism at times. Searching for any logical answer to explain this conundrum of events. Again there was the three week window or timeline from my initial intuitive thought regarding the accident and the event actually occurring – why? How could I have known? Surely if we examine logic and the ratio of chance and risk it would have told us this accident although possible was not probable or likely to happen – wouldn't it?

I cannot answer the reason why? or how? precognitive dreams or intuitive thoughts present as they do in our lives thus affecting our whole being. There is a vastness to our unknown universe that knows no bounds. Taking us with it into new dimensions and experiences. Past, present and future tenses explored – like on the fine tuning of a radio wave connecting earthly minds – Oh forgive me! A bit deep isn't it.

I only know that it seems real for me in my life.......

❖ ❖ ❖

L ittle Dee - as we call her - is one of my many nieces. She had just turned twelve years old and is the second daughter of my younger sister. Dee is one very brave and extremely lucky little girl I can tell you. All of her family are glad

that she is still with us today. I will explain.........
I experienced a strange but lucid dream about Dee
only a few months ago now. Her face came to me in
my sleep likened to an image on a photograph. I had
no idea why I was dreaming about her. She seemed
blissfully happy and carefree and was sat astride
her cycle waiting to set off down the road with her
friends.

> *It reminded me of a picture dad has of my sister
> at pretty much the same age and in a similar
> situation. She was sat astride her cycle, hap-
> pily posing with friends outside our old house
> on Fotherby road before setting off on her bike.
> I remember it was summer and she was wear-
> ing a bright yellow sleeveless tee-shirt in her
> photo.*

The connection I felt to both images was the happy
emotions both mother and daughter were experiencing. Young and innocent with not a care in the
world! This I sensed and felt with them - it was divine. In reality life had been thwart with difficulties
for both of them recently and due to circumstance
Dee had gone to live with her older sister.

The next image in my dream was suddenly of Dee
in a deep sleep and not able or wanting to awake.
She was dressed in the same clothing as the previous
image from what I can remember but her eyes were

closed and she lay completely still. I looked around in my dream for any clues as to where she was – Dee was in the most beautiful grass meadow fast asleep. Long soft lush green grass with wild flowers surrounded her. A glorious warm summer day with a very gentle breeze floated by her. Her hands were across her chest holding onto some flowers – daisies, I think. There was such a peaceful calm and tranquility about the place and Dee although deep in sleep was smiling – she didn't seem to want to move from here? A sleeping beauty. I sensed she felt safe and happy here because it connected her to lost loved ones and happy memories.

I tried desperately to wake her because I knew she couldn't stay. It wasn't her time. My efforts to rouse her were to no avail and I awoke abruptly from my sleep feeling bewildered at what I had just seen and witnessed. What did it all mean? Unfortunately, the answer to this question I was soon to discover!

A few weeks later, I was sat in my conservatory at home feeling tired and exhausted from a difficult shift at the hospice and was reflecting on the events of the day. I suddenly, received an urgent text from my niece (Dee's older sister) asking me to contact her. It was around six o clock in the evening, I remember. I had no anticipation of the events that were about to unfold. I telephoned her immediately.

Little Dee had been involved in a car accident and

was seriously ill. My neice informed me that Dee was being transferred from Grimsby hospital to the Children's hospital in Sheffield. Intensive Care Unit. She had been with friends outside the house playing. They were on bicycles. Dee had just gone down the driveway into the main road and had not seen the oncoming car. She was knocked off her bike as the vehicle hit her and she had landed on the concrete. Dee had sustained a life threatening head injury and suffered altered conscious levels. In intensive Care (ICU) she was put into an induced coma. Her family were told that the next twenty four hours were crucial and to expect the worse. My neice wanted me to let Granddad Foster know about the accident. I was devastated at this news as were all the family.

I think we all felt a little helpless and knew her fate was out of our hands. I have never prayed and cried as much as I did that evening. My main concern after my dream was that Dee would not want or be able to wake up from whatever place she had gone to in her subconsciousness. I hoped her love for her family and longing for the physical plane was strong enough to bring her back to us. Dee had experienced difficulties in her complicated life already at such a young age due to family circumstances – what more were she going to have to endure – how unfair, it all seemed for my sister and her family to have to go through this now!

I sensed she was lost somewhere between this

world and the next. I had never quite believed in miracles before. Dee had been given a less than ten percent chance of survival. All the odds seemed to be against her recovering. I prayed that evening for my mother Barbara Rose (Dees' grandma) to bring her back to us. I thought if anyone could find her wandering spirit it would be her. Human faith brought us through this ordeal. I can't say it was particularly religious but for me it was certainly spiritual and I am sure it was for her family.

Little Dee went on to make a miraculous recovery. Within a week she was conscious and breathing without the aid of a ventilator. She was transferred back to Grimsby hospital and after a few days was allowed to go home. A very lucky and loved little girl much to the relief of her family.

So I ask myself? Was my dream precognitive? Was it a warning about the accident? Or was it just merely a dream? I can honestly answer that I have no idea! The only comfort I have is in ourselves as a family unit. A dysfunctional one at times. We were able to come together at the point of crisis and display the human faith and spirit it holds within it. We have our mother's love instilled within us and passed through the generations to thank for that!

APPARITIONS.

Wikipedia, the free encyclopedia; (don't you just love Wiki) describes an apparitional experience as an "anomalous, quasi-perceptual experience and is characterized by the apparent perception of a living being or inanimate object without any material stimulus for such a perception." The person experiencing the apparition is fully conscious and awake. The term ghost suggests; that some element of the human being survives death and can make them perceptible to living human beings.

Scientific investigations into Psychical Research have taken place for many years with the likes of Gurney, Myers and Podmore and they strived to provide evidence for human survival after death. Myers also examined the theory of Telepathy and was able to provide valuable data concerning the phenomenology of hallucinations in the sane – the ability to prove survival of death remains controversial even today.

..... Lots of big words then – but still no full explanation – but in truth who knows for sure if ghosts or spirits exist anyway– unless of course they have seen one!

If we tell others we may have had these experiences then the tendency is fear of ridicule.

None of us want to be teased or laughed at or made a complete idiot of do we? For this reason in itself I feel that many of us choose to remain silent about our experiences. It would be a shame if millions of people throughout the world are experiencing extrasensory perceptions in whatever form they may take and are unable to be honest about it to others. All that knowing and not the telling. We all sit silent afraid of repercussions. All those connections waiting to be made between what we can see and what we cannot – but human nature unfortunately often fears the unknown!

Well thank goodness more people are "Coming out" so to speak. Ironically, it is the achievements of science in its physical form through the development of computers and the internet that are providing the connections for humankind to speak out about their experiences at last. There are now many websites and digital downloads of applications or books about extrasensory perception, dream visitations, apparitions, telepathy, the sixth sense, the astral plane and so on.....At some point in our lifetime we will surely learn and accept that all of the sciences are interconnected with not just our physical being but our soulful beings. What could be more holistic than that? We are not only a sum of our parts our parts make up the whole – think I read that somewhere.....

Apologies for digressing. I think the original question was have I had any apparitional experiences – the answer is yes. I will tell you about these now........

I believe I have seen probably three or perhaps four spirits so far in my lifetime. My previous experiences as a child of visiting the Astral Plane – I truly believe this happened to me – has allowed me to have occasional connections with those who have recently died and are passing over into this realm. The spirits I have borne witness to have mostly been at this stage of their transgression. That is my belief. In biblical terms this is called ascension of the Holy Spirit. You know when Jesus showed himself to his disciples after his crucifixion before he ascended to Heaven. I suspect the astral plane is a bit of a "pit-stop" before moving on. In alien terms it means "beam me up Scotty"..... Sorry couldn't resist just having a bit of fun with you. It is the place your soul goes to before ascending to the higher realms – that is if you believe in their existence in the first place. I have to confess this theory is kind of growing on me.

I cannot discuss these experiences in chronological order for reasons which shall become clear later......

◆ ◆ ◆

My mother Barbara died on Valentine's Day in 2009 at the age of sixty five. She was a wonderful mum, always supportive and there for us. I miss her every day!

I remember mum being poorly for the last fifteen years of her life. Diagnosed eventually with emphysema and at a young age, by all accounts, but the consequence was still the same. Already enduring her symptoms with great dignity she required continuous oxygen via a concentrator for last several years of life. Unable to get upstairs she slept downstairs in a recliner chair for years. Dad had a stair lift installed and adaptations around the house but mum was set in her ways. She struggled to lay flat so the chair was the easier option. However, she was still able to rule the roost even from that damned chair!

Had a bit of a chuckle to myself remembering that.....

Then came the double "Whammy" A new doctor sent mum for a chest x-ray because of her reduced air entry into her lungs. I wish even now she had not had this done – there was no point. Already informed she was at final stages of her emphysema she knew her time was short. Mum was then confirmed to have lung cancer. Whereas, she had accepted the emphysema she was in denial about the cancer right until the end – she never came to terms with the unfairness of it and this brought out anger in her at times – understandably of course – but it seemed mostly aimed at me. In hindsight, I think with my nursing background mum thought I could provide some miracle cure to save her but of course I couldn't. Unfortunately she was already frail and in essence dying from the emphysema and so not able to tolerate any chemotherapy or surgery. It was not an option. We continued to look after mum and palliate her symptoms with input from the Macmillan Nurse.

Mum wanted to die at home and in the end she got her wish. I had discussed the hospice with her but she preferred home with her family. It was a bloody nightmare trying to get her into an electric profile bed which was required for the last three weeks of her life – stubborn as an ox clinging on to her independence at all costs. I wouldn't have wanted her to be any other way. The last twenty-four hours of her life and since have been understandably tearful and emotional as our grief unfolded. But I must explain the strange events that occurred to you......

I had decided to take time off from work to be with my family and look after mum. The day before she died she was semi-comatose and had a syringe driver with a small amount of sedation due to the partial seizures she had been experiencing. She looked comfortable and peaceful. I had noticed a change in her breathing pattern at teatime – but my intuition and gut feeling told me I must stay with her and not go home – I knew her time was fast approaching although not imminently. Eventually; dad went to bed for a few hours as he was exhausted. My sister and I kept a bedside vigil.

At about 3.30 in the morning, I felt a presence in the room. I had been "catnapping" in the other recliner chair and my sister was asleep on the settee. I felt a whoosh... as something passed by me. It looked like a person's legs moving dressed in what appeared to be grey flannel trousers. I jumped up feeling a bit scared and woke my sister to say what I'd seen – not sure if she believed me really but bless her she didn't question it. You see, I always knew that if someone were to come for mum to take her from this world into the next it would be her father Granddad Hunt and guess what! He always wore grey flannel trousers.....imagine that! I also felt that Uncle Brian (mums brother who died young) was with us at that time.

By 5.30 am dad was downstairs and we had called our other siblings to attend. Mums heart was stronger than we thought but she eventually slipped away peacefully a few hours later - holding her youngest daughters hand as she had made her promise to do so and took her last breathes on earth. I saw her change in appearance as her soul left her physical body leaving her face looking younger and relaxed with almost a smirk across her lips. But even so as a family we fell apart at our loss and took console in each other. Dad needed his own space and wandered down the garden.

At 2.00 pm I made my way home. My heart feeling heavy. I had used all my reserve and energy trying to hold it together for the sake of my family. I felt so emotionally drained and had nothing left to give. I had wanted to resolve some issues with mum about her diagnosis but did not get the chance as things happened so fast. I felt she was angry with me for some reason: possibly because, I was the one who couldn't promise to keep her at home if dad was not coping; although, I promised to try my best. Thankfully in the end home was where she was able to be for her last days of life.

I cried inconsolably all the way home. I don't know how I managed to drive the car. All I could think about was that she had been angry with me and I never got the chance to explain – in my emotional high I found myself talking to her asking her forgiveness and telling her how much I loved her and would miss her. I immediately felt a presence in the car. Once inside my house I stood tearful in the corner of my kitchen.

I was drying away the tears from my eyes and I looked up near the notice board and mum was suddenly there! Still wearing the blue nighty she had passed away in. She was smiling at me but didn't speak – but there was no need for words as I strongly sensed her love. Her face was clear but only for a few seconds and has my tears flowed she faded like a mist as quickly as she had appeared. Thank you for that mum xxxx. Mum wasn't alone someone or something was stood at her side holding onto her hand as though guiding her but they just appeared as a grey form I couldn't make them out or didn't want to because I only wanted to see my mum........

Yes! I believe I did see the spirit or ghost of my lovely mum. I think my own natural energy both physical and spiritual drew her back to me for a few moments in time. It was a wonderful experience and one I shall never forget.

Of course mum hasn't left her visits there as I will explain further..........although her visits are not in the form of apparitions but in other ways.

The following day which was a Sunday I was deep in grief and crying on and off all day – as I know were the rest of my family. We felt our loss was immense but each of us also needed our own space and time to grieve privately in our own way. Looking at a particular photo of mum. It was one of those precious moments we had on a holiday in Cornwall quite a few years earlier and we were both dressed in orange tee-shirts (as Virgo's we often picked the same colour clothing to wear and used to laugh at this – very uncanny).

I spoke to my mum in the photo; crying emotionally wishing I could just hear her voice again and be able to tell her how much I loved her, when the telephone rang. This startled me making me jump a little as I wasn't expecting any calls via the landline at that precise time. I picked up the receiver and initially thought it must be a wrong number as the line was dead and nobody answered. Then suddenly a loud static noise bellowed in my ear and I could just make out a very faint voice and the odd word. I could hear a scrambled voice saying "Andrea" albeit very quietly and as my family all know I am a bit deaf as well as daft at times. This lasted for quite a few minutes until eventually the "white noise" stopped sounding and the normal tone of the telephone returned. How strange, I remember thinking. We had never experienced any problems with the phone before.....

I dialled the 1471 number to check who had just rang or indeed to see if it was a call at all or perhaps a fault on the line. I was still endeavoring to look for a logical answer. It confirmed that there had been a telephone call but the number was unknown! Heck I thought, was it a crank call or something wrong with the line? I checked the phone was in normal working order and it was.

So! It seems that just for a few fleeting minutes when my emotions were high and my longing and yearning to hear mums voice was foremost in my mind that someone, somewhere was somehow attempting to make that connection with me via the telephone. Trying not to over think this dilemma or letting my imagination run wild.....

Of course, I had to ask myself that question – could the static noise on the other end of the phone have been mum trying to make that connection with me when I needed her most? Do I honestly believe in that stuff? The timing of the call. The emotions I was experiencing. It was just one coincidence to many – could it be even possible! Without wanting to appear a total nincompoop! I opted for the logic convincing myself it was a fault on the telephone line..... In hindsight and with other similar experiences since this event – I guess I will never know for sure.....It does give me some comfort thinking it might have been mum trying to contact me despite how odd or perhaps disconcerted it may seem.

*There are of course other ways to make con-
nections with lost loved ones and one way is
through dream visitations – that is if you believe in them?*

A few months after my mum had passed away I was
still struggling with coming to terms with my loss.
I had a great fear of forgetting what she looked like
and constantly surrounded myself with pictures of
her. Eventually after some time this burden eased
and I surrounded myself with happy memories and
images. The one thing I missed terribly was her
touch. She had always been a very tactile person as
I am myself. I very selflessly missed her not being
at home sat in her recliner chair reaching and holding my hand when I sat down beside her – this was
comforting to me and now it was gone! I remember thinking," If only I could feel her touch on my
hand once more"....This thought plagued me for the
next couple of days affecting my sleep at night and
I found it increasingly unsettling. I missed her so
much.

I need not have concerned myself because true to
form mum visited me in a dream that night......
I found myself walking into mum and dad's lounge
and there she was sat in that old black recliner
chair. She turned towards me and smiled saying,"
don't worry, Andrea I'm still here, I haven't gone
anywhere". I sat down next to her and she reached

out and held my hand just like she used to patting it gently. My goodness it felt so real. I could feel the warmth of her touch with her hand on mine. The sense of love, comfort and reassurance I felt was amazing and overwhelming. Just what I envisaged and desperately needed at that stage of my grief – thank you for that mum! Love you always!

> Interestingly, I recently read a book by Jacky Newcomb called Heaven (2013). She tells numerous stories about the general public's experiences of the afterlife. Jacky is considered a leading expert on the afterlife and knows the spirit world is real. She continues that thousands of people have experienced spontaneous contact with loved ones as they appear in dreams and visions after they have passed over. Her evidence has been gathered over the last thirty years from the many people that have written testimonials about their own personal experiences and encounters. Within her conclusion of the book and after conducting her own research she states, "I am completely convinced that the soul continues as a living personality-energy after physical death. Death of the physical body is not the end of life".

After much soul searching and my own personal experiences of the afterlife, I feel inclined to agree with her to some extent. Life can't be all logic and reason – can it?

◆ ◆ ◆

A few years ago now Andy and I went to stay in Scarborough for a couple of days. We stayed in one of those old private hotels on the north cliff face on the other side of the castle. They are Victorian four and five storey houses and have much history. I cannot for the life of me decide if this next true event was a dream visitation, ghostly apparition or a out of body experience – perhaps it was all three if that is remotely possible.....

We had been neatly placed on the very top floor in what I intuitively felt must have been the old attic area or a onetime nursery. It was pleasantly decorated and furnished but I sensed a past presence immediately on entering the room. It wasn't too uncomfortable but if I'm honest it was slightly foreboding. I decided not to let it ruin our little holiday and got on with the unpacking. Probably just my senses being aware of the oldness and past history of the property or so I tried to convince myself.

After a lovely day out visiting Scarborough's sights

we returned late evening and settled into bed quite exhausted as we had walked miles. Andy was soon in a deep sleep and snoring as usual. I eventually drifted off into my slumber. I thought, I had awoken but found myself looking down at the bed and I was asleep in it. (another out-of-body experience). Running around the bed were three small children. Two little girls and a small boy. All had blond curly hair and were laughing and giggling playing around my bed. The strange thing was their attire. The children could not have been more than three, four or five years old and they were all dressed in black Victorian funeral clothing.

They tried to wake me up by tickling my nose and prodding my face not harshly but playfully. This, I could clearly see, as my spirit floated above us all. Andy was fast asleep and ignorant of events. I sensed the children had lost a parent and the day I was witnessing had been a funeral. I remember envisaging a horse and carriage outside and it may have been the funeral hearse. These small children were not sad because they were too young to understand the situation.

I fell back into my body very suddenly with a jolt and remember feeling quite annoyed at the noise the little ones were making as I was so tired. I sat up in bed still sleepy and shouted out "Andy! Will you tell these bloody kids to be quiet I'm trying to get some sleep" I vaguely remember Andy muttering something and then I fell back into a deep sleep.

When I awoke it was a bright fresh morning and the sun was shining and yes I remembered everything from what I thought had been a dream? I instinctively knew that the room we were in had been the children's nursery and that was why they behaved in that fashion. We were intruding on them! On a funnier note Andy did recall me shouting out and said to me "What were you going on about telling the kids to be quiet?" I explained the night's events and as usual he just rolled his eyes at me...........

Ever walked into a room and just for a split second thought that you had seen people sat there and then on your second glance back there was no one......just an empty room? I'm sure many of you will have had this experience at some point in your lives. Of course our tendency is to brush it off as if it hadn't happened at all or to blame it on our over-active imaginations – isn't that human nature?

We tell ourselves to believe only what you can see on the physical plane. Any other explanation would be absurd! But what would you do if when you took that second glance back you did see other people in that same room. How would you know if they are real or just ghostly apparitions? Unless of course they said, "BOO!"

Whilst I was at work – this very scenario occurred. I had always felt many presences in the lounge of the hospice but never actually seen anything to write home about. It wasn't an eerie feeling by any means I just became very aware of lingering souls. Sometimes, even they like to jest about a little. On more than one occasion on a late shift I would walk through the lounge into the reception area and see people sat in the recliner chairs and I remember looking straight back – on that second glance – and the room being empty. I did what we all do and convinced myself not to be so silly. However, if I had wanted true affirmation of spirits in the lounge it was indeed going to happen soon.

On one particular evening shift I was walking through the lounge area and for what seemed like ages the room was full of people sat in the chairs smiling at me. I was shocked because some of them I had been nursing and had recently passed away. I smiled at them and I think I even said, "Hello" just as it would have been on a normal day unit day at the hospice. The lounge was bright and the sun shone through the conservatory. I walked through until I reached the door on the far end of the lounge and I then remembered it was late evening and the day unit was closed – on my second glance back the room was empty!

So what do you make of that. Dammed if I know either!....................

◆ ◆ ◆

I may not have seen many ghostly or spiritual apparitions but the ones I have were quite sur-real. However; this next experience was wit-nessed by more than one person and so gives it a little more credibility. I shall explain..... I had just completed a night shift and handed over to my nurs-ing colleagues on the morning shift. Once changed out of my uniform and into my day clothes I was ready for home. I signed out as per the norm for fire regulations and made my way into the car park. Something or someone caught my eye as I glanced to my right.

A man dressed in a light blue shirt and darker blue trousers was facing me. He looked middle aged and his hair was dark and wavy; slightly longer into his neck although brushed over his ears. The first thing that struck me as odd was his attire – no coat? it was chilly and there had been an early morning frost. The man didn't say anything. He was a safe distance away on the grassed area to the left of the main entrance. His movements were not normal they appeared very slow as if he was floating just above the ground. I could see his feet, he had black shoes on but they didn't seem to be touching the grass at all. It was like he was actually walking on air.

I became frightened and started to freak out a little. Quickly, I jumped in my car and started the engine up. My heart was racing. My colleague who left work at the same time drove past first and gave me a friendly wave as she went on her way – she seemed not to see the man at all. The man turned slowly to face me. Resting on his arm was a double barreled shot-gun! It was "Half-cocked" I presumed open because it was not in use.

I felt petrified but my instinct told me he was not here to harm anyone and I didn't feel it was me he was searching for. What to do? Run inside and tell everyone? When they probably wouldn't be able to visualize the guy anyway........ I plucked up the courage to drive slowly past him. Whilst doing so I chanted to myself " OH! Andrea stop being silly ".... You know they often get the local farmer in early mornings, occasionally to keep tabs on the wild rabbits. That is probably what he was doing? Rabbit cull..... Yes, I know crazy or what!

Driving past him he turned around slowly to face the main road. It was as if he was in his own protective bubble and his feet were definitely not touching the ground. I could clearly see this now. Was I being shown a glimpse of his parallel universe or was he gently stepping into mine? I recognized him as a previous patient and thought he must have only recently passed over and so was still in the transgression stage of his ascension from this world into the next. He was lingering for a purpose. Although, I knew he meant me no harm I still sensed it was not me he was waiting for. I continued on my journey home and was well in need of my bed and sleep.

How on earth I managed to settle after that experience I honestly do not know but I suspect it was the sheer physical exhaustion of the night shift and the ghostly sighting. If ever I had doubted the existence of spirits, ghosts – call them what you will – then this experience certainly relinquished those thoughts from my mind. As far as I was concerned at this point in my life – spirits and ghosts do exist – I had seen it for myself!

Imagine my surprise when I discovered I was not the only person to see this apparition on that same day. In the same place and pretty much at the same time as a collegue. I have never discussed my experiences openly, only with a few close members of my immediate family. For several months neither my work collegue or I mentioned the visitation to anybody. I mean who would believe us – in saying that neither of us knew about each other's sighting of the same man. Until, one early shift my colleague and I went for break together for the first time in ages.

Often this is just how the off duty works out. Kerry (not her real name of course) suddenly began to tell me about her sighting of the man. Same time, same place and in the same way as he appeared to me. No expression or emotion on his face I recall. Kerry agreed with that also.

Whereas, I couldn't remember the person it seemed she did. She knew his name and when he died. Kerry had lengthy conversations with this person and had got to know him very well. I then remembered this gentleman myself and recalled how we had cared for him and his family. It seems Kerry had set him a challenge. The subject matter went something like this: Kerry "Well I will believe it when I see it. Once you've gone that's it. If you can prove me wrong then find a way to return and show me, then I will believe that there is something more" Or words to that effect. This kind and lovely man agreed to do this if he could. He would find a way to let her know if there is life after death for our souls. What a deep discussion it must have been.

She went on to explain to me that the gentleman had been a Gamekeeper for many years and they had spoken about his work at length, mainly reminiscing. So that explained, why he held his gun aloft in his arm as though he was working the land and had many happy memories of that time in his life. So it all started to make sense at last. I remember, Kerry came into morning handover quite breezy and ruffled but it never crossed my mind it was because

she had seen a ghost! Small world isn't it then.........
Two people can't be completely wrong can they?
To have shared the same exact experience. How bizarre is that. Surely this event has to contain an element of credibility.

Are you becoming more convinced? If not I think the next event I am about to discuss will shock even you. I can assure you it certainly did me at the time.

It has taken over two decades to truly believe it actually happened but I can assure you all it did! I was unable to tell you about this visitation first or in a true chronological order because of its nature. If I have managed to enlighten you to become more insightful then hopefully I may have gained your trust. I could not tell you more otherwise. Please read on ....

◆ ◆ ◆

I remember being at home with my family and feeling quite lamentful and thankful for my life and for having my two wonderful children in it. It was my thirty- fifth birthday. An age when one starts to take "stock" of life events I think – perhaps for the first time. The children where in bed contently snoozing and my husband was watching television in the front lounge. I chose to dwell in the dining room watching a late night movie whilst enjoying a glass of wine to celebrate my birthday – well ok - two glasses then! Certainly no more than that as I have always been somewhat of a lightweight in the alcohol department.

I finally took my leave and went upstairs to my bed at around 00.30 am gone midnight. I settled into a light sleep and could feel myself drifting off into a deeper reverie. I felt peaceful and calm within myself as I snuggled down.

Suddenly, a short while after, I awoke gasping for breath clutching my chest. I remember putting my right hand on my chest and feeling an immense crushing pain. I managed to pull myself onto my elbows in bed and eventually after what seemed like forever, caught my breathe and inhaled deeply. Upon exhalation my pain, panic and fear appeared to leave me as if it had jumped out of my chest via my mouth when I exhaled. I was then physically able to sit up in bed. No pain and no breathlessness. What an earth was that all about? I remember asking myself. Surely not my heart or angina at my age? But it had felt as though for a brief while my heart had stopped beating!

Still clutching my chest I glanced upwards towards

the end of my bed and there she was. Just stood staring down at me. I blinked a few times and rubbed my eyes to ensure I was fully awake and not dreaming. Nope, definitely wide awake now! What the heck! She was dressed in a three quarter beige jacket – or so it appeared. That was clearly visible to me. Her body and legs were in black garments. I couldn't see all of her legs or feet only just to below her knees. Initially her face was clear and I recognized it immediately – oh my god what is she doing here in my room at the end of my bed? Her blonde hair was its usual neatness and she looked beautiful but it was those big blue eyes which were now sullen and void of life and the sadness in her face that gave her away. I have to say, it crushed my heart again emotionally this time.

And then I knew. I had felt her physical pain and now I was tuned in to feeling her emotional pain. The sadness she felt at being cheated of life. She was not ready to leave! Her pain was for her children – and I think this is where we connected somehow – one mothers love to another...........Once I had seen her clearly and had felt her pain and emotion the visual image of her soul started to fade as though she was being pulled back to the here and now. I instinctively knew she had been visiting the astral plain – that place between this world and the next – but why? Was she also capable of having out of body experiences in her dream state I wondered?

At this point I glanced at my clock on the bedside

cabinet and because I usually set it half an hour fast – force of habit I'm afraid – I had to calculate the time. It was approximately a few minutes before 1 am in the morning. You have to remember at this time I was oblivious to the events that where to unfold later that day. I sat upright in bed for what seemed like an eternity. Right, so what has actually just happened here? It wasn't a dream. I'm totally alert and fully conscious! And then it hit me the ultimate question – what the hell! was the Peoples Princess doing stood at the end of my bed at this time in the morning and why was she so desperately sad? I could never in a million years have anticipated the devastating news that was already circulating in the media and press at that point..........

What to do? Do I need to go to hospital to get checked out after my physical experience of chest pain? Wouldn't that be the sensible thing to do? Who would believe me! Should I go downstairs and explain to my husband the events that have occurred – no! not a good idea because he doesn't really believe in such unearthly sightings and visionary experiences. I continued to do what was customary for me at that time in my life and pulled the duvet up under my chin and attempted to get back to sleep. Effectively, "burying my head in the sand" to another life affirming experience just because I didn't truly believe in myself enough to tell the world. I knew it would be a very long time before I could do that.........

Later that morning I awoke early and went downstairs to get a cuppa and some breakfast. The rest of the family were still asleep. I turned on the television in the dining room and listened to the news. I was profoundly and deeply shocked to hear that the Princess of Wales had died as a result of injuries sustained in a car accident in Paris. It was August 31st 1997. My birthday had been the day before. She was barely a year older than me – I felt an unbearable pain at her loss as did everyone – my heart went out to her family and especially her boys.

I will never know why she visited me that night and I have strived to make some sense of the dilemma over the years – the only thing I understand with certainty is that she wanted someone to witness her pain and emotional sadness at leaving this world as she felt it wasn't her time to go. I wasn't sure what else I was supposed to do for her.........

The only person I have ever felt confident to discuss these events with is my daughter – but hey! She thinks I'm a bit of a weirdo anyway – so nothing new there then. I did, what I always do, and filed the experience away somewhere safe. Not forgetting it of course but neatly placing it in one of the folders in that never opened steel cabinet somewhere in the back of my mind. Over the years that have followed the Princess of Wales death and the intrigue surrounding the circumstances in which she died; I too had many unanswered questions. This has caused me emotional turmoil at times – the preverbal what if's – I had done something or told someone – but in all honesty I know deep down in my heart that there was nothing physically more I could have done for her, other than being a witness to her emotional sorrow and anguish – feeling her pain and her loss – in the end at least in that she was not alone.........

It has taken me a long time to come to terms with this event and to now openly speak of it – for all the obvious reasons. I've never wanted or encouraged media limelight and that is true even now. Please remember this is my story and life journey. I have only now chosen to share it with you. This experience was a significant force in waking me up to my true potential because I started to believe in myself from that point on.

I still needed to lay my emotions to rest regarding the episode and finally find some peace within myself about the whole affair. For this reason my daughter agreed to go with me to visit The Princess of Wales ancestral home of Althorpe on the tenth anniversary of her death. The many visitors would provide a blanket of warmth to hide myself within. I am so glad I made that journey. Whilst I was sat in her monumental gardens I felt the most exquisite peace and tranquility. The sun was shining and a gentle breeze passed through and I felt that we where both at last at peace with the world..........she was back in the loving arms of her family.

May God Bless You,

If I had written this first would you have ever believed me? Perhaps you don't even now? One thing
is for sure, eventually....... the truth will out!

THE INTERLUDE

I must now confess that, although, I have found writing about my experiences quite difficult at times, it has been somewhat therapeutic in a strange way that I cannot explain.... But as we all know the reality of life often stops us in our tracks as we go about our usual mundane tasks on a daily basis. I struggled to continue to write further and seemed to find endless excuses not to continue or the preverbal "Save the book for a rainy day – who will be interested anyway?" period was back. I am afraid self-doubt had silently crept in again.

For the last couple of years, I have enjoyed precious time with my family and constantly worked hard in my professional area of nursing – palliative care – I never seemed to have time to do anything else or an inclination to start writing again until recently........But life has a funny way of throwing strange "curveballs" at us doesn't it sometimes?

And I am now in a place in my life that has strangely ensured I can commit some much needed time and energy to this book. It is has though; I have been given some time-out to concentrate on this project. I now know I need to finish what I have started in order to move forward myself in my own life. So how has this revelation come about I hear you asking?......

A very odd thing happened to me about eight or nine weeks ago now. I received a letter to attend for my routine mammogram being a lady of a certain age. I read the date on the letter to attend but that specific date didn't seem to register with me. I seemed to sense I needed to go on the Wednesday a week before the actual appointment time. I read the letter several times but only ever saw the date I had in my head which was a week early – I didn't think I was losing my marbles because in my head this was the date I kept seeing on the letter. I organized to leave work early to attend.

As I approached the steps leading up to the mobile unit at our local hospital I decided to check the date on my appointment letter. The letter was for the following Wednesday and I was in fact a week early. I couldn't believe I had read the letter wrong. Why was I convinced I needed to be here now? I conducted very regular checks on myself and had felt no breast lumps? Feeling rather silly at myself I returned to work and attended on the correct date the following week. Even at this point I never considered anything was really wrong. In hindsight, I think my body was trying to tell my brain I required this scan done sooner rather than later – perhaps? After just six days of having the mammogram done I received my "call-back" letter to attend for further tests. I was eventually diagnosed with Ductal invasive primary breast cancer. Thankfully, a small lump (never felt it) and I was reassured it was very early stages. To cut a long story short – I feel as though I have been to Hell and back! Okay, probably a little too dramatic for a description.

I have certainly had a taste of the raw emotions, shock, disbelief and eventually acceptance that comes with a diagnosis of this nature. You just think this happens to someone else don't you? The big "Why me" question seems to have no one answer. In hindsight, I consider myself to be very lucky that my cancer was found early on and is treatable – many brave people I have cared for over the years where not so – and although I am eternally grateful to the Universe picking up on this "curveball" at the right time to enable treatment and cure – I am also; very aware of those poor souls who have gone before and have not been so lucky. This cuts me to the core! I just hope that my own experiences of cancer enables me to be an even more understanding empathetic nurse and practitioner. Otherwise; what was the point of my cancer? I want to return to a job that I love – Hospice care.

So? I find myself in an unreal situation whilst I

am in-between treatments. I had my surgery three weeks ago. Wide local incision and Sentinal lymph node biopsy. Physical healing seems slow and the mental torture of waiting for biopsy results is agonizing. How blessed am I that amongst all the chaos and grief of the last two months I have received some good news at last. The four lymph node biopsy's where clear – thank God! I feel like I have been given a second chance at life. I am presently awaiting Oncology to discuss my further treatment plan. I have been informed that the most likely treatments are radiotherapy and hormone therapy probably Tamoxifen.

Of course I know I am "not out of the woods yet" but things are looking more positive. There will however; always be the niggle at the back of my mind about cancer spread and recurrence. I guess I just have to learn to live with that as do all other cancer survivors. Survivorship never sounded so great!

Here's the weird conundrum – I always, knew I would end up with a cancer diagnosis – I have no idea why?

Logically because of the fact I have lived in passive smoke all of my life. First with my mother and then my husband – along with other age relating factors and being overweight, menopausal – oh! The list is endless. I thought I was high risk of perhaps lung cancer and had convinced myself it was likely no matter how much I avoided the smoke I would probably end up with this. I have no family history of breast cancer what-so-ever? Lots of new research lately on the connection with cancer and sugar. Unfortunately I have a very sweet tooth. Not sure what to make of it really and maybe I shouldn't read more into it that there actually is. That is wisest I think! I do feel that someone or something out there was looking out for me though – thank you! Guess that is an odd thing to say after being given a cancer diagnosis but it could have been much worse than it is. Only the passage of time will tell...

Nope ! I am afraid to say; I did not manage to write more at that stage. On a positive note; I concentrated on getting well after surgery and radiotherapy treatment and returning to work after six months continuing to do the job that I love. Hospice nursing. Many colleagues have asked me; how do I manage to carry on working in this environment given my own diagnosis of breast cancer – my answer is this......Yes, it is difficult at times, especially emotionally, but I now have true empathy with my patients. I know what it feels like to be given a life changing diagnosis. The bubble you withdraw into whilst life goes on around you. The fear of waiting for test results. The fear of recurrence. Questioning my own mortality. Who decides who lives and who dies? Deep shit isn't it !

So for the last two years I have gotten on with my life. Throwing myself into my work and concentrating on my family. Of course as we get older and our remaining parents become less agile and we have had to take on extra responsibility in caring for them which I suspect has taken its toll on my health but I love my dad to bits and would not have it any other way. So where do I fit the kids and grandchildren in I hear you asking? Not easy is it – not enough hours in the day sometimes however; I have always been good at multitasking thank goodness!

So here comes another "curveball" A couple of weeks ago I had some abnormal vaginal bleeding. I am presently on hormone treatment to reduce the risk of the cancer returning and so should not have this symptom. My GP in her wisdom "fast-tracked" me for a suspected gynecological cancer which resulted in a hysteroscopy under general anaesthetic and a large endometrial polyp being surgically removed. I am reassured by the consultant that on screen it doesn't look anything sinister but am sat waiting patiently for biopsy and histology results. It feels a little like – here we go again – certainly no "déjà-vou" moment this time as did not see this one coming.

Alas, I tell myself, "There for the grace of god go I" What will be will be. But the truth is I'm only 57 years old and I want more time with my

*family – do I have the right to ask for that in the great scheme of things; well probably not – lots of people much worse off than me – I know that is true and I am thankful for each day truly I am but a few more won't hurt either. Okay......
That's my justification and affirmations sorted then.*

So, I have some time whilst off from work to relook at this book or journal – call it what you will - I don't mind , honestly. I want to attempt to get back on track. Correction I will get back on track! I am determined to do so.......

We will continue with my next experience of intuitive precognitive dreams.

Interlude over:

◆ ◆ ◆

This is probably going to be the most difficult one to explain and I suspect that due to the emotional turmoil it has caused me over the last twenty or so years, I have continuously avoided dealing with it.......... (time to change that).

ember at the beginning of this book I told you that some of my precognitive dreams where quite distressing as they involved the loss of loved ones and the last thing I wish to do is cause more heart-ache to any living soul. Especially if a loss has involved a child...I say a personal little prayer before I go to sleep for my family and especially my son and daughter and more recently for my grandchildren. Since this precognitive experience I chant this simple prayer for all children. This is my prayer/mantra and I say it every night before I go to sleep.

> *"God bless everyone in the whole wild world and especially the little children. Please keep them all well, safe and happy and above all please save them their innocence. Amen.*

THE CHILDREN.

The Dream

The front door of a house I do not recognize slams shut! I am outside. Everything around me appears to be in a dull khaki-green colour. The front door, my clothes and my surroundings. It feels like me but when I look down at my hands and turn them upwards I see they are not mine. They are the hands of a man. In my dream state, I immediately realize I am trapped inside this person's body and unable to wake up. I feel frightened – usually with this level of fear and emotion I bring myself out of my dream and back to reality but he won't let me – he wants me to see this – why? I can feel his emotions. He is angry so very angry! He wants to teach them all a lesson? Who? Whatever is happening to this man I have tuned into his raw emotions and I do not like what I am feeling.

The man slammed his front door shut but it felt as

though I had done this.

I am looking through his eyes. I am in his body. I rush down the steps from the door and out into the street It is in tunnel vision. I can only see slightly to the sides and what is directly in front of me. I try to look around to get my bearings – a road sign – anything to tell me where I am – but he won't let me – he is so angry and focused and full of intent – nothing is going to stop him We are almost marching not running but still moving with speed. As I look down at his body I see his arms and legs moving – left, right, left, right swinging his arms. We continue marching up the street I think we passed some green railings.

Abruptly, we stop. I am now inside a building. He knows this place. It is familiar to him. He knows exactly where he is going. He takes a deep breath – the anger within him is overwhelming and all consuming – I have never felt anything like it in my life! Still within him I feel petrified. I can't get out. I want to get out......dear god please help me.....Once he has taken a breath he turns left and hurriedly walks on. I am looking down a corridor with windows down the sides. At the end of this corridor we turn right and enter into a large room. It reminds me of the dining room we used to use as a gym when I was at infant and junior at my old school in Haxey. Lots of long wooden benches like we had at school. This memory fills me with some warmth but he doesn't feel this warmth. There is only anger and deep rage within him – he is past saving.

It is noisy in this room. I glance up and through his eyes I see many little children girls and boys and at a guess I would say infants. All laughing and cheerful. All happy and enjoying gym class or P.E as we used to call it. .....Why are we here?....

He comes to a halt. (I am within him.) I see what he sees. I feel what he feels. But my own emotions are still within me. I want to be free of him! I don't like what he is making me feel. He has no regret and no remorse. He feels a nothingness – I don't know how to explain it to you... this feeling of dread!

A beautiful little boy with blonde hair and I think blue eyes recognizes me (him). The child is dressed in a white vest tee-shirt and black gym pants/shorts. He recognizes me and seems happy to see me. He is on the wooden bench and turns around to face me smiling and says; Hello, Mr ....Bang! ...I look down at my hands (his hands) and I am holding a black revolver gun...I wake up suddenly from the dream gasping for breath and crying uncontrollably. Tears streaming down my face. I am free of this man at last and the relief of this burden hits me like a sickening punch in the gut because it felt as though, I had pulled the trigger. No! No! No! I scream inwardly it is just a dream. Why would anyone ever want to do such a thing? It wasn't real. What a horrible nightmare to have.

I continued to tremble my whole body shaking and

tentatively climbed out of my bed without disturbing my husband and went down stairs to recover from the shock and horror of this ordeal. I needed to allow myself some time to make some sense of the things I had witnessed and find a way to deal with my emotions.

I had no understanding at this point of what this dream meant and why it had felt so real. I remember being quite traumatized by it. Could I stop something like this from happening – who would believe me anyway? It was just a dream – right! Throughout the next couple of weeks I constantly watched the news channels and checked daily papers searching for this man but I didn't really know what he looked liked or where he lived even if he did exist. It is a vast world out there and it was like looking for a "needle in a hay stack" But I was determined to try. Of course it was to no avail because I had very little information to go on and please remember I had much self-doubt in myself and my ability to see into the future at this time in my life. I did not understand what was happening to me or why I was being shown these images especially when they were so random and I had no control over them.

Logically my brain was telling me it must be an horrendous haunting dream and nothing more but my gut and intuition were not convinced. Due to the nature of this event, I decided to conducted my own research about such things in order to aid my own understanding and find some practical solutions to deal with the emotional trauma it was causing me. This experience had a major impact on my mental and physical health. It was all consuming and drained me of my energy and life force (spirit). It dawned on me that these experiences came at a cost not only to others but to myself. They drained you of life and aged you at the same time. I could not afford to let this happen as I still had a very young family. Could I find a way to block these random dreams and intuitive thoughts.

It was this particular precognitive experience that eventually led me to believe in my so called "three week window" into future events .This was the timescale and hand the universe had dealt me and within the next few weeks I was to find out how the truth would unfortunately unfold............

The tragedy of the Dunblane children in Scotland hit the headlines approximately three weeks later. I think it was on BBC news first and then I remember watching Lorraine Kelly on the morning breakfast show paying tribute herself and reporting the horrific episode of events. I instinctively knew this was it – my dream was the beginning of his murder spree. I had not had the spiritual strength to stay with him through it all. I could barely cope with the images I had seen. My god so many innocent young children had died in this blood bath and at the hands of this monster. I rushed out to buy daily papers for more information. I knew for certain when I saw a picture of the offender in the daily papers that it was definitely him. I didn't need to know what he looked like I could still feel him and his miserable, condescending presence. Seeing the later pictures of the children was overwhelming and especially so of one particular little blonde haired boy....

God bless all the brave little children.........and please deliver us from evil......Amen.

It was a devastating and tragic incident which affected many and my thoughts and prayers are forever with the families of these young children taken so brutally young in life.

I have other stories to tell but I think this is a poignant place to stop writing for now about my precognitive experiences and dreams. I have tried to inject some humor into my grammar at appropriate times and that is just me being me. A coping mechanism I think.

The pain of what we see and feel in our dream state – "hits you" doesn't it? When our interpretations of our stories seem real or actually become real in our own lives or those of others around you who you may not even know or have never met.

TO CONCLUDE:

*I want to take you back
to the beginning!*

Remember; what I said about precognitive dreams and thoughts and how it feels for me. It's like a fine tuned frequency or radio wave – we all have them – I think, what happens is we just accidently jump onto each other's radio wave from time to time and see things through the mind's eye of that person. Perhaps this radio wave is innate and we have just forgotten how to use it to connect with each other? It might be something from our genetic makeup of our past e.g survival "fight or flight" or something which is developing for us to use in the future e.g. telepathy.

Science and Spirituality need to evolve together. Spirituality is our life force – our soul being and that which connects us to each other and all life on earth and in the vast universe – Science is our way of learning in the physical plane. Science and Spirituality together become holistic and encompass all elements of the mind, body and soul. Eventually; acquisition and acceptance of this knowledge and concept will then allow us to travel soulfully through the universe and its various realms both physically and mentally. Time travelling may well be the "fifth" element we have yet to discover whether it be with our bodies or with our minds.

The ability to be a good person or an evil person remains in us all I guess and as you know there are lots of theories about that. I don't presume to have all the answers and in fact I continue to ask many questions myself about why things happen to us in life - good or bad.

Individually; we can only be the best that we can and do the best that we can.

If we can't do anything else; then just be true to yourself and kind to others.

Thank you for reading.

REFERENCES

1. Wikipedia. 2011. Astral Plane. (Online) Available at: http://en.wikipedia.org/wiki/Astral_plane. (Accessed 30 July 2011).

2. Mystical Empowerment. 2011. The Astral Plane. (Online) Available at: http://www.mysticalempowerment.com/astral_plane.htm (Accessed 30 July 2011).

3. StLyrics. 2011. Judy Garland. Somewhere over the rainbow. (Online) Available at: http://www.stlyrics.com/lyrics/thewizardofoz/somewhereovertherainbow.htm (Accessed 16 September 2011).

4. Wikipedia. 2013. Apparitional experience. (Online) Available at: http://en.wikipedia.org/wiki/Apparitional_experience (Accessed 8 February 2013).

5. Dreams.org 2011. Dreams - String Theory. Quantum physics. (Online) Available at: http://www.dreams.org.es/ (Accessed 31 July 2011).

6.   Wikipedia.   2011.   Death   of   Diana,Princess   of   Wales.   (Online)   Available at: http://en.wikipedia.org/wiki/Death_of_Diana_Princess_of_Wales (Accessed 30 July 2011).

7. BBC Home. 2011. On this Day. 1997: Princess Diana dies in Paris crash. (Online) Available at: http://news.bbc.co.uk/onthisday/hi/dates/stories/august/31/newsid_2510000/2510615.stm   (Accessed 30 July 2011).

8.   Princess-Diana.com 2011. Accident - Princess Diana's Accident. (Online) Available at: http://www.princess-diana.com/diana/accident.htm (Accessed 30 July 2011).

9.   Wikipedia. 2011. De'ja' vu. Scientific research and related phenomena. (Online) Available at: http://en.wikipedia.org/wiki/D%/C3%A9j%C3%AO_vu (Accessed 31 Julu 2011).

10. BBC Home. 2011. On this Day, 1996: Massacre in Dunblane school gym. (Online) Available at: http://bbc.co.uk/onthisday/hi/dates/stories/march/13/newsid_2543000/2543277.stm (Accessed 30 July 2011).

11.   BBC-h2g2. 2011.   The Dunblane Massacre. (Online) Available at: http://www.bbc.co.uk/dna/h2g2/A11103580 (Accessed 30 July 2011).

12. Guardian.co.uk. 1996. Eriend Clouston and Sarah Boseley. Dunblane Massacre (Online) Available at: http://century.guardian.co.uk/1990-1999/Story/0%2C6051%2C112749%2C00.html (Accessed 30 July 2011).

13. Wikipedia. 2011. Dunblane Massacre. Timeline of event. (Online) Available at: http://enwikipedia.org/wiki/Dunblane_massacre (Accessed 30 July 2011).

14. Wikipedia. 2011. Precognition. (Online) Available at: hhtp://en.wikipedia.org/wiki/Precognition (Accessed 31 July 2011).

15. Wikipedia. 2011. Intuition (Knowledge) . (Online) Available at: en.wikipedia.org/wiki/Intuition_(Knowledge) (Accessed 31 July 2011).

16. Wikipedia. 2011. Extrasensory Perception. (ESP) J.B.Rhine. (Online) Available at: http://en.wikipedia.org/wiki/Extrasensory_perception (Accessed 31 July 2011).

17. Newcomb.J. (2013) Heaven. Incredible true stories of the afterlife. Penguin publishing.

AFTERWORD

Towards the end of this book, I have dedicated a few blank pages, to you my readers, so that you too can write about your own dreams or intuitive thoughts. I suggest; that you keep this book at your bedside to enable you to access it quickly. If you awake from a dream that you have remembered and want to write about it in note form, then use the following few pages to do so....

You never know you may be
inspired to keep your own
journal of dreams............

◆ ◆ ◆

ABOUT THE AUTHOR

Andrea J Parker

I am a professional nurse who has found her vocation in palliative care nursing and hospice work. I have a loving family who continue to support me through my experiences in life and I am eternally grateful to them. I hope I have shown a true and honest version of myself and with that in mind have have achieved some credibility in my written work.

My Dreams:

Date and Time:

Subject:

My Dreams:

Date and Time:

Subject:

My Dreams:

Date and Time:

Subject:

Printed in Great Britain
by Amazon

18678156R00058